Memories of the Heart

By Joan Walsh Anglund

Memories
of the
Heart

by

Joan Walsh Anglund

Random House New York

Library of Congress Cataloging in Publication Data

Anglund, Joan Walsh.
Memories of the heart.
I. Title.
PS3551.N47M4 1984   811'.54   83-21251
ISBN 0-394-53576-6

Manufactured in the United States of America

9 8 7 6 5 4 3

For
Sharon Winter

Though time forgets
still love remembers

The Puzzle of Life
      has many pieces,

      but only one
      solution.

Love, alone,
    . . . solves all riddles

    . . . answers all questions

      . . . silences all doubts.

Upon stone,
       is written fact.

Upon parchment,
       is written wisdom.

. . . Upon the human heart,
       is written Love.

Belief

is at the beginning

of all accomplishment.

We speak

of the same Sea

. . . though we stand

on separate Shores.

How sure
    are the Seasons,

How steady
    is Time

    . . . and yet
       . . . more constant than these

       is

       Love!

Love

    cannot speak

till
  Self
    is silenced.

How comforting

    to know

each word

    . . . or silence

      is understood.

For,

    often,

      words say less

than

    the silence

      that lies between

        two who Love.

Death

    is the fear

    that we shall no longer *be.*

Love

    is the knowledge

    that we do not die!

This Shell

    is

empty

    of the Life

      it

        held . . .

and yet,

    how exquisite

      are its hollows.

And in the end,

    are we not *all*

      such hollows

. . . shaped

    by the Loves

      that once

        filled us?

All rivers

    come, at last,

        . . . to the Sea.

All pain

    comes, at last,

        . . . to Peace.

All fear

    comes, at last,

        . . . to Love.

All spirit

    comes, at last,

    home again

        . . . to God.

Wisdom is

    as the morning light

. . . a gradual

    illumination.

There is

no harder lesson

than Loneliness.

Without a star

     to guide,

Would we not

     all

       lose our way

       in the Darkness?

Without a friend

     for comfort,

Would not Despair

     engulf

       the most steadfast

         among us?

We must not ever forget

    that we are sisters

       . . . that we are brothers

       . . . that we are a family

    brought here

       to help

         one another!

The Memories

    of the Heart

        are the warmest embers.

Thought is the work

of the Mind,

as

Love is the occupation

of the Spirit.

Love never locks,

> it frees.

Possessiveness

> is not Love.

It is Fear

> . . . afraid of losing

that

> which it can never

> own.

Be ashamed

       to say you love

unless

       you also

           forgive.

The Past
is a faraway land

. . . to which

we

can never return.

Faith whispers

in the heart

of every Dream.

Love

    is a candle

in the Darkness.

By its light

    we shall find

        our way.

What a dream

      . . . is this little Self.

What a reality

      . . . is the eternal Spirit.

Though time

forgets,

Still,

love

remembers.

The journey of Love

is long

. . . and does not stop

at Death.

Prayer

    is the pathway

Stillness

    is the Temple

Love

    is the offering we bring

Peace

    is the gift

        we are given.

What shall we hold

    tomorrow,

  but

    the love

     we gave

      . . . today?

Let my heart ever be open

> to the Beauty
>> of others,

> to the Sorrow
>> of others,

> to the Need
>> of others,

> to the Love
>> of others.

Let me lose my Self

> in the service
>> of others,

that I may more surely

> fulfill
>> Life's purpose.

Let me forgive

> all men their anger,

> and all men their differences,

>> that they may forgive me mine,

so that each, blameless,

> we may join,
> as equals,
>> in the unity of Love.

To all things

there is

an ending

. . . to Love

. . . there is none.

JOAN WALSH ANGLUND, the much-loved author-artist of such celebrated titles as *A Friend Is Someone Who Likes You* and *Love Is a Special Way of Feeling*, lives with her family in an eighteenth-century house in Connecticut. Her books, whose sales number in the millions, have been widely published, and include editions in England, Germany, Sweden, Denmark, Norway, Spain, Brazil and South Africa.